THE LIBRARY (

IRISH
MUSIC

MW00800491

AMSCO PUBLICATIONS
NEW YORK/LONDON/PARIS/SYDNEY

COMPILED BY AMY APPLEBY

ORDER NO. AM 945681
US INTERNATIONAL STANDARD BOOK NUMBER: 0.8256.1653.0
UK INTERNATIONAL STANDARD BOOK NUMBER: 0.7119.6771.7

EXCLUSIVE DISTRIBUTORS:
MUSIC SALES CORPORATION
257 PARK AVENUE SOUTH, NEW YORK, NY 10010 USA
MUSIC SALES LIMITED
8/9 FRITH STREET, LONDON W1V 5TZ ENGLAND
MUSIC SALES PTY. LIMITED
120 ROTHSCHILD STREET, ROSEBERY, SYDNEY, NSW 2018, AUSTRALIA

PRINTED IN THE UNITED STATES OF AMERICA BY
VICKS LITHOGRAPH AND PRINTING CORPORATION

CONTENTS

The Wearin' o' the Green

Traditional

7

The Harp That Once thro' Tara's Halls

Words by Thomas Moore

Traditional Air: "Gramachree"

Erin, Oh Erin

Words by Thomas Moore

Traditional Air: "Thamama Hulla"

1. Like the bright lamp that lay on Kil - dare's ho - ly fane, And burn'd thro' long
2. The na - tions have fall - en, and thou still art young, Thy sun is but
3. Un - chill'd by the rain, and un - wak'd by the wind, The lil - y lies

1. a - ges of dark - ness and storm, Is the heart that sor - rows have frown'd on in
2. ris - ing, when oth - ers are set; And thro' slav - 'ry's cloud thy morn - ing hath
3. sleep - ing through win - ter's cold hour, Till the hand of spring her dark chain un -

1. vain, Whose spir - it out - lives them, un - fad - ing and warm; E - rin, oh
2. hung, The full moon of free - dom shall beam round thee yet! E - rin, oh
3. bind, And day - light and lib - er - ty bless the young flower, E - rin, oh

1. E - rin, thus bright thro' the tears Of a long night of bon - dage thy spir - it ap - pears.
2. E - rin, tho' long in the shade, Thy star will shine out when the proudest shall fade!
3. E - rin! thy win - ter is past And the hope, that liv'd thro' it, shall blossom at last.

The Minstrel Boy

Words by Thomas Moore

Traditional Air: "The Moreen"

Not too slow

1. The min-strel boy to the war is gone, In the ranks of death you'll find him; His
2. The min-strel fell! but the foe-man's chain Could not bring his proud soul un - der; The

fa - ther's sword he has gird - ed on And his wild harp slung be - hind him. "O
harp he loved ne'er spoke a - gain, For he tore its chords a - sun - der; And

Land of Song!" said the war - rior bard, "Tho' all the world be - trays thee, One
said, "No chains shall sul - ly thee, Thou soul of love and bra - v'ry, Thy

sword at least thy rights shall guard, One faith - ful harp shall praise thee!"
songs were made for the pure and free, They shall ne'er sound in sla - v'ry!"

When Irish Eyes Are Smiling

Words by Chauncey Olcott & George Graff, Jr.

Music by Ernest R. Ball

sweet lilt-ing laugh-ter's like some fair-y song, And your eyes twink-le
spring-time of life is the sweet-est of all, There is ne'er a real

bright as can be; _____ You should laugh all the while and all
care or re-gret; _____ And while spring-time is ours through-out

oth-er times, while, And now smile a smile for me. _____
all of youth's hours, Let us smile each chance we get. _____

CHORUS

When I-rish eyes are smi-ling, ___ Sure it's like a morn in

Spring.____ In the lilt of I - rish laugh-ter, You can hear the an - gels sing.____ When I - rish hearts are hap - py,____ All the world seems bright and gay,____ And when I - rish eyes are smi - ling, Sure they steal your heart a - way. When way.____

The Kerry Dance

Words by James Lyman Molloy

Based on "The Cuckoo" by Margaret Casson

1. Oh, the days of the Ker-ry danc-ing! Oh, the ring of the pi-per's tune!
2. Was there ev-er a sweet-er Col-leen In the dance than Ei-ly More!

Oh, for one of those hours of glad-ness, Gone, a-las! like our youth, too soon!
Or a proud-er lad than Tha-dy As he bold-ly took the floor!

When the boys be-gan to gath-er In the glen of a sum-mer night,
"Lads and lass-es to your pla-ces, Up the mid-dle an' down a-gain,"

And the Ker - ry pi - per's tun - ing Made us long_ with wild de - light:
Ah! the mer - ry heart - ed laugh - ter Ring - ing through the hap - py glen!

rit.

meno mosso — *rall.*

Oh, to think of it, Oh, to dream of it, fills my heart with tears!

a tempo

Oh, the days of the Ker - ry danc - ing! Oh, the ring of the pi - per's tune!

rit.

Oh, for one of those hours of glad - ness, Gone, a - las! like our youth, too soon!

a tempo — *p più lento*

Time goes on,__ and the hap - py years are

mf a tempo — *p più lento*

16

Erin! the Tear and the Smile in Thine Eyes

Words by Thomas Moore

Traditional Air: "Aileen Aroon"

Dublin Bay

Words by Annie Barry Crawford

Music by George Barker

1. They saild a-way in a gal-lant bark, Roy Neal and his fair young
2. Three days they saild when a storm a-rose, And the light-'ning swept the
3. On the crowd-ed deck of that doom-ed ship Some fell in their meek de-

1. bride, They had ven-tur'd all in that bound-ing ship, That danc'd on the sil - v'ry
2. deep, When the thun-der crash broke the short re-pose Of the wea-ry sea boys
3. spair, But some more calm with a ho-lier lip, Sought the God of the storm in

1. tide; Roy Neal he clasp'd his weep-ing bride, and he kiss'd the tears a-
2. sleep; Roy Neal he clasp'd his weep-ing bride, and he kiss'd the tears a-
3. pray'r; "She has struck on a rock!" The sea - men cried, in the breath of their wild dis-

1. way, And he watch'd the shore re - cede from sight of his own sweet Dub - lin Bay.
2. way, "O love, 'twas a fear-ful hour," he cried, When we left sweet Dub - lin Bay."
3. may, And that ship went down with that fair young bride, That saild from Dub - lin Bay."

Killarney

Words by Edmund O'Rourke

Music by Michael William Balfe

1. By Kil - lar - ney's lakes and fells, Em - 'rald isles and
2. In - nis - fal - len's ru - in'd shrine May sug - gest a
3. No place else can charm the eye With such bright and
4. Mu - sic there for Ech - o dwells, Makes each sound a

1. wind - ing bays, Moun - tain paths, and wood - land dells,
2. pass - ing sigh, But man's faith can ne'er de - cline
3. va - ried tints; Ev - 'ry rock that you pass by,
4. har - mo - ny; Man - y voic'd the cho - rus swells,

Come Back to Erin

Words & Music by Claribel
(Charlotte Alington Barnard)

The Dear Little Shamrock

Words by Andrew Cherry

Music by W. Jackson

The Birth of Saint Patrick

Words & Music by Samuel Lover

Now the first faction fight in owld Ireland, they say,
Was all on account of Saint Patrick's birthday;
Some fought for the eighth, for the ninth more would die,
And who wouldn't see right, sure they blacken'd his eye!
At last, both the factions so positive grew,
That *each* kept a birthday, so Pat then had *two,*
Till Father Mulcahy, who show'd them their sins
Said "No one could have *two* birthdays, but a *twins.*"

Says he, "Boys, don't be fighting for eight or for nine,
Don't be always dividing, sometimes combine;
Combine eight with nine—seventeen is the mark—
So let that be his birthday." "Amen," says the clerk.
"If he wasn't a twins, sure our hist'ry will show
That, at least, he's worth any two Saints that I know!"
Then they all got blind drunk, which completed their bliss,
And we keep up the practice from that day to this.

O'Donnell Aboo

Traditional

Wildly o'er Desmond the war wolf is howling;
    Fearless the eagle sweeps over the plain;
The fox in the streets of the city is prowling—
    All who would scare them are banish'd or slain!
      Grasp every stalwart hand,
      Hackbut and battle brand;
Pay them all back the deep debt so long due;
      Norris and Clifford well
      Can of Tyrconnell tell,
Onward to glory, "O'Donnell Aboo!"

Sacred the cause that Clan-Connaill's defending,
    The altars we kneel at and the homes of our sires;
Ruthless the ruin the foe is extending,
    Midnight is red with the plunderer's fires.
      On with O'Donnell, then,
      Fight the old fight again,
Sons of Tyrconnell all valiant and true,
      Make the false Saxon feel
      Erin's avenging steel!
Strike for your country "O'Donnell Aboo!"

The Daughters of Erin

Words by Thomas Moore

Traditional Air: "Garryowen"

nev - er need leave our own __ Green Isle, For sen - si - tive hearts and for
warns the touch while win - ning the sense, Nor charms us least when it
bil - lows of woe and beams _ of joy, The same as he look'd when he

sun - bright eyes.
most _ re - pels. } Then re - mem - ber, wher - ev - er your gob - let is crown'd, Thro' this
left _ the shore. }

world wheth - er east - ward or west - ward you roam, When a cup to the smile of dear

wom - an goes round, Oh! re - mem - ber the smile which a - dorns her at home.

The Cruiskeen Lawn

Traditional

hap - py night and day With my charm - ing lit - tle cruis - keen
glass shall ne'er run dry, Nor my smil - ing lit - tle cruis - keen
Bac - chus gave me leave To take an - o - ther cruis - keen

lawn, lawn, lawn, With my charm-ing lit - tle cruis - keen lawn.
lawn, lawn, lawn, Oh! my charm-ing lit - tle cruis - keen lawn.
lawn, lawn, lawn, To take an-oth - er cruis - keen lawn.

CHORUS.

's Gra-machree ma cruis-keen, Shlan-the gal ma-vour-neen,'s Gra-machree a cool - een

bawn, bawn, bawn, Oh! 's Gra-machree a cool - een bawn!

St. Patrick's Day

Words by Thomas Moore

Tune from Playford's *Dancing Master*

33

Oh! Steer My Bark to Erin's Isle

Words by S. Nelson

Music by T. Haynes Bayly

Let Erin Remember the Days of Old

Words by Thomas Moore

Traditional Air: "The Red Fox"

The Bells of St. Mary's

Words by Douglas Furber

Music by A. Emmett Adams

sound of the sea, I know you'll be wait-ing, yes wait-ing for me. The
voi-ces shall sing, For you and me dear-est the wed-ding bells ring.

REFRAIN

Bells of St. Ma-ry's, Ah! hear they are call-ing The

young loves— the true loves Who come from the sea, And

38

young loves — the true loves Who come from the sea, And so, my be -

lov - éd, When red leaves are fall - ing, The love-bells shall ring out — ring out For

you and me. you and me.

Where the River Shannon Flows

Words & Music by James I. Russell

fair - ies and the blar-ney Will —— nev - er nev - er die. It's the
bless the ship that takes me To my dear old Er - in's shore. There I'll

land of the shil - lal - ah, My heart goes back there dai - ly To the
set - tle down for - ev - er I'll leave the old sod nev - er, And I'll

girl I left be - hind me When we kissed and said good - bye.
whis - per to my sweet-heart, "Come and take my name As - thore."

Chorus.

Where dear old Shannon's flow-ing, Where the threeleaved Shamrock's grows, Where my heart is I am go-ing, To my lit-tle I-rish rose. And the moment that I meet her With a hug and kiss I'll greet her, For there's not a col-leen sweet-er, Where the Riv-er Shan-non flows.

Down by the River Lee

Words & Music by Adam O'Neill

44

In the Valley Near Slievenamon

Words & Music by Daniel J. Sullivan

1. A - lone, all a - lone, by the wave-beat-en strand, All a - lone in the crowd - ed
2. It was not the grace of her dear charm-ing face, Nor her cheeks like the ros - es' red
3. A - lone, all a - lone, by the wave-beat-en strand, Sad and wea - ry my lone spir - it

hall;_____ The hall is so gay and the waves are so grand, But my
glow;_____ Oh, blame not the eyes nor her tress - es so fair, Nor__
cries:_____ "My love, oh, my love, will I see you no more? And my

Isle o' Dreams

Words by George Graff, Jr.
& Chauncey Olcott

Music by Ernest R. Ball

Dear Harp of My Country

Words by Thomas Moore

Traditional Air: "New Langolee"

free _ dom, and song! The warm lay of love and the
worth _ y than mine, If the pulse of the pat _ ri - ot,

light notes of glad _ ness Have wak - en'd thy fond _ est, thy
sol - dier, or lov - er, Have throbbed at our lay 'tis thy

live - li _ est thrill; But so oft hast thou e - choed the
glo - ry a - lone; I was but as the wind pass - ing

deep sigh of gladness, That ev'n in thy mirth it will steal from thee still.
heed - less-ly o - ver, And all the wild sweet-ness I wak'd was thy own.

Danny Boy

Words by Frederick E. Weatherly

Traditional Air: "Londonderry Air"

Oh, Dan-ny Boy the pipes, the pipes are call-ing _ From glen to glen, and down the moun-tain side, _ The sum-mer's

But when ye come, and all the flow'rs are dy - ing,___ If I am dead, as dead I well may be,_____ Ye'll come and find the place where I am ly - ing,___ And kneel and say an A - ve there for me;___ And I shall

cresc. *sempre legato.* *dolce.* *espress.*

Molly Malone

Traditional

father and moth-er were fish mon-gers too, They

drove wheel-bar-rows thro' streets broad and nar-row, Cry-ing

"Cock-les and mus-sels, a - live all a - live!"

colla voce

rit.

62

Sweet Rosie O'Grady

Words & Music Maude Nugent

name is Rose O' Gra - dy and, I don't mind tell - ing you, That
on her fin - ger that I placed a small en - gage - ment ring, While

she's the sweet - est lit - tle Rose the gar - den ev - er grew.
in the trees, the lit - tle birds this song they seemed to sing!

CHORUS. Valse.

Sweet Ro - sie O' Gra - dy, My dear lit - tle

Rose, She's my stea - dy la - dy,

65

Rory O'More

Words & Music by Samuel Lover

I'll Take You Home Again, Kathleen

Words & Music by Thomas P. Westendorf

Macushla

Words by Josephine V. Rowe

Music by Dermot MacMurrough

blue - eyed Ma - cush - la, I hear it in vain.

Ma - cush - la! Ma - cush - la! your white arms are reach-ing, I

feel them en - fold - ing, ca - ress - ing me still. Fling them out from the darkness, my

lost love, Ma - cush - la, Let them find me and bind me a - gain if they will

8

Has Anybody Here Seen Kelly?

American Version by
William J. McKenna

Words & Music by
C.W. Murphy & Will Letters

74

Mary's a Grand Old Name

Words & Music by George M. Cohan

77

Peg o' My Heart

Words by Alfred Bryan

Music by Fred Fischer

Oh! my heart's in a whirl, Ov - er
When your hearts full of fears, And your

one lit - tle girl, I love her, I love her, yes, I
eyes full of tears, I'll kiss them, I'll kiss them all a -

heart fond - ly sighs,_ as I sing to her eyes,_ Her eyes of
light of love shine_ from your eyes in - to mine,_ And shine for

blue, _____ Sweet eyes of blue, my dar - ling!
aye, _____ Sweet - heart for aye, my dar - ling!

poco rall.

REFRAIN

Peg O' My Heart, _____ I love you, We'll nev - er part, _____

p-f

8va

I love you, dear lit - tle girl,_ Sweet lit - tle girl,_

8va

Sweet-er than the rose of Er - in, are your win-ning smiles en-dear-in', Peg O' My Heart,_____

Your glan - ces with Ir - ish art_____ en - trance us,

Come, be my own,— Come, make your home_ in my heart._____

heart.

Kathleen Mavourneen

Words by Annie Barry Crawford

Music by Frederick W. Nicolls Crouch

1. Kath - leen Ma - vour - neen! the grey dawn is break - ing,___ The horn of the
2. Kath - leen Ma - vour - neen! a - wake from thy slum - bers!___ The blue moun-tains

1. hunt - er is heard___ on the hill; The lark from her light wing the
2. glow in the sun's___ gold-en light; Ah! where is the spell that once

1. bright___ dew is shak - ing, Kath - leen___ Ma - vour-neen!___ what, slum - b'ring
2. hung___ on my num - bers? A - rise in___ thy beau-ty,___ thou star of my

1. still!
2. night.

Oh, hast thou for - got - ten how
Ma - vour - neen, Ma-vour-neen, my

1. soon we must sev-er? Oh, hast thou for-got-ten this day we must part? It
2. sad tears are fall-ing, To think that from E-rin and thee I must part? It

may be for years, and it may be for-ev-er; Oh, why___ art thou

si-lent, thou voice of my heart? It may___ be for years, and it

may be for-ev-er; Then why___ art thou si-lent, Kath-leen Ma-vour-neen?

Little Annie Roonie

Words & Music by Michael Nolan

Harrigan

Words & Music by George M. Cohan

I'm just as proud of my name you see, As an Em-per-or, Czar or a
la-dies and ba-bies are fond of me, I'm fond of them, too, in re-

King, could be: Who is the man helps a
turn, you see: Who is the gent that's de-

man ev-'ry time he can? Har-ri-gan, That's me!
ser-ving a mon-u-ment? Har-ri-gan, That's me!

CHORUS. SOLO.

CHORUS.

H - A - dou-ble R - I - G - A - N spells Har-ri-gan,

87

Proud of all the I-rish blood that's in me; Div-il a man can say a word a-gin me. H - A - dou - ble R - I - G - A - N, you see,_____ Is a name that a shame nev-er has been con-nect-ed with. Har-ri-gan, That's me!__ me.__

Molly Bawn

Words & Music by Samuel Lover

Mol-ly Bawn, why leave me pin-ing, All lone-ly wait-ing here for you? The

mo-ther, Na-ture, set them sleep-ing, With their ro-sy fac-es wash'd with dew.
knows I'd steal you, Mol-ly dar-ling, And then trans-port-ed I should be. } Oh!

stars a-bove are bright-ly shin-ing, Be-cause they've no-thing else to do. Mol-ly

Bawn! Mol-ly Bawn! Now the Bawn!

MacNamara's Band

Words by John J. Stamford

Music by Shamus O'Connor

* 3rd and 4th Verses sung one after the other without refrain

92

O Katy O'Neil

Words & Music by Edward Rupert

95

Savourneen Deelish

Words & Music by George Colman, Jr.

When the word of command put our men into motion,
    Savourneen Deelish, Eileen oge!
I buckled my knapsack to cross the wide ocean,
    Savourneen Deelish, Eileen oge!
Brisk were our troops, all roaring like thunder,
Pleased with the voyage, impatient for plunder;
My bosom with grief was almost torn asunder,
    Savourneen Deelish, Eileen oge!

Long I fought for my country though far from my true love,
    Savourneen Deelish, Eileen oge!
All my pay and my booty I hoarded for you, love,
    Savourneen Deelish, Eileen oge!
Peace was proclaimed; escaped from the slaughter—
Landed at home, my sweet girl I sought her,
But sorrow, alas! to her cold grave had brought her,
    Savourneen Deelish, Eileen oge!

Terence's Farewell

Traditional Air:
"The Pretty Girl Milking Her Cow"

Words by Lady Dufferin

It's a folly to keep you from goin',
    Though, faith it's a mighty hard ease!
For Kathleen, you know there's no knowin'
    When next I may see your sweet face!
And when you come back to me, Kathleen,
    None the better shall I be off then;
You'll be spakin' sich beautiful English.
    Sure, I won't know my Kathleen agen!

Eh, now! what's the need of this hurry?
    Don't fluster me so in this way!
I've forgot, 'twixt the grief and the flurry,
    Every word I was manin' to say!
Now, just wait a minute, I bid ye!
    Can I talk if ye bother me so?
Och! Kathleen, my blessin' go wid ye,
    Every inch of the way that you go!

Norah, the Pride of Kildare

Words & Music by John Parry

1. As beauteous as Flo-ra Is charming young No-rah, The joy of my heart and the pride of Kildare: I
2. Where'er I may be, love, I'll ne'er for-get thee, love, The beauties may smile, and try to ensnare: Yet

ne'er will deceive her For sad-ly 'twould grieve her To find that I sigh'd for an-o-ther less fair: Her
no-thing shall ev-er My heart from thine sev-er, Dear No-rah, sweet Norah, the pride of Kildare: Thy

heart with truth teeming, Her eye with smiles beaming, What mortal could in-jure a blossom so rare As
heart with truth teeming, Thy eye with smiles beaming, What mortal could in-jure a blossom so rare As

No-rah, dear No-rah, the pride of Kil-dare, Oh, No-rah, dear No-rah, the pride of Kil-dare.

Kate Kearney

Words by Lady Morgan

Traditional Air: "The Beardless Boy"

1. Oh, did you not hear of Kate Kear - ney? She
2. For that eye is so mo - dest - ly beam - ing, You
3. Oh! should you e'er meet this Kate Kear - ney, Who
4. Tho' she looks so be - witch - ing - ly sim - ple, Yet there's

lives on the banks of Kil - lar - ney, From the glance of her eye, Shun
ne'er think of mis - chief she's dreaming; Yet, oh! I can tell How
lives on the banks of Kil - lar - ney, Be - ware of her smile, For
mis - chief in ev - er - y dim - ple; And who dares in - hale, Her

dan - ger and fly, For fa - tal's the glance of Kate Kear - ney.
fa - tal the spell That lurks in the eye of Kate Kear - ney.
ma - ny a wile Lies hid in the smile of Kate Kear - ney.
sigh's spi - cy gale, Must die by the breath of Kate Kear - ney.

Mother Machree

Words by Rida Johnson Young

Music by Chauncey Olcott
& Ernest R. Ball

Allegretto, ma espressivo.

There's a   spot   in me heart which no   col - leen may own, There's a
Ev - 'ry sor - row or   care in   the   dear days gone by, Was made

depth in me soul nev - er   sound - ed or   known; There's a
bright by the light of the   smile in your   eye; Like a

place in my mem - 'ry, my life, that you fill, No
can - dle that's set in a win - dow at night, Your

molto rall.

oth - er can take it, no one ev - er will.
fond love has cheered me, and guid - ed me right.

molto rall.

Tenderly with much expression

Sure, I love the dear sil - ver that shines in your hair, And the

mp espress.

brow that's all fur - rowed And wrin - kled with care. I

kiss the dear fin - gers, so toil - worn for me, Oh, God

bless you and keep you, Moth - er Ma - chree!

She's the Daughter of Mother Machree

Words by Jeff T. Nenarb

Music by Ernest R. Ball

104

Father O'Flynn

Words by Alfred Perceval Graves

Traditional Air: "The Yorkshire Lasses"

1. Of priests we can of-fer a charm-in' va-ri-e-ty, Far re-nown'd for *larn-in'* and pi-e-ty;

1. Still, I'd ad-vance *ye wid-out* im-pro-pri-e-ty, Fa-ther O'Flynn as the flow'r of them all.

CHORUS

Here's a health to you, Fa-ther O'Flynn, *Slain-té and slain-té and slain-té a-gin;*

Pow'r-ful-est preach-er, and ten-der-est teach-er, And kind-li-est creat-ure in *ould* Don-e-gal.

* Pronounced "Slawntia" meaning "your health"

107

Peggy O'Neil

Words & Music by Harry Pease,
Edward G. Nelson & Gilbert Dodge

Nellie Kelly I Love You

Words & Music by George M. Cohan

John James O'Reilly

Words & Music by Emma Carus,
J. Walter Leopold & Herman Kahn

that big and strong, He let's noth-ing go wrong, Sure he stops the whole
don't want to boast, We'll live bet-ter than most, And still save ov-er

world with one hand_____ When the girls they go by prom-en-
half of his pay_____ For my man has an eye on the

ad-ing_____ Smile up at him as sweet as can be_____ But he
fu-ture_____ And has hopes we wont have to wait long_____ Till a

pays no at-ten-tion, I just want to men-tion, He's
sweet lit-tle ba-by, Or two of 'em may-be, Can

114

Mickey Donohue

Words by Irving Kaufman,
Jack Kaufman & Frank Williams

Music by Frank Hughes
& George B. McConnell

116

The Last Rose of Summer

Words by Thomas Moore

Traditional Air: "The Groves of Blarney"

The Pretty Girl Milking Her Cow

Traditional Air: "Cailin Deas"

1. It was on a fine sum-mer morn-ing, The birds sweet-ly tuned on each bough, And
2. Then to her I made my ad-van-ces; "Good-mor-row, most beau-ti-ful maid, Your
3. "The In-dies af-ford no such jew-el, So bright and trans-par-ent-ly clear; Ah!

as I walk'd out for my pleas-ure, I saw a maid milk-ing her cow; Her
beau-ty my heart so en-tran-ces!"Pray, sir, do not ban-ter," she said; "I'm
do not add flame to my fu-el! Con-sent but to love me, my dear." Ah!

voice so en-chant-ing, me-lo-dious, Left me quite un-a-ble to go, My
not such a rare pre-cious jew-el, That I should *en-am-or* you so, I
had I the lamp of A-lad-din, Or the wealth of the A-fri-can shore, I'd

heart it was load-ed with sor-row, For *Col-leen dhas cru-then na moe.
am but a poor lit-tle milk-girl," Says Col-leen dhas cru-then na moe.
rath-er be poor in a cot-tage With Col-leen dhas cru-then na moe.

*) Irish.Trans:- The pretty girl milking her cow.

Oft in the Stilly Night

Words by Thomas Moore

Traditional Air

Affettuoso

The Girl I Left Behind Me

Words & Music by Samuel Lover

The Rose of Tralee

Words by C. Mordaunt Spencer

Music by Charles W. Glover

My Beautiful Irish Maid

Words & Music by Chauncey Olcott

Remember Thee

Words by Thomas Moore

Traditional Air

My Wild Irish Rose

Words & Music by Chauncey Olcott

'Tis an Irish Girl I Love
(And She's Just Like You)

Words by J. Keirn Brennan & Alfred Dubin

Music by Ernest R. Ball

I found that trea - sure, so pre - cious and rare, that my heart___
Just how I've longed for the time she'd be mine, You know well___

___ will a - dore._____ Not a duch - ess nor a
___ who I mean._____ Sure, she has your eyes of

queen, She's just like your - self, my col - leen._____
blue, She al - ways re - minds me of you._____

rit.   a tempo

REFRAIN

Girls are girls in Lon - don - der - ry, In Kil - ken - ny,

p-f

133

A Place in Thy Memory

Words by Gerald Griffin

Traditional Air: "The Hard-Hearted Maiden"

Love's Young Dream

Words by Thomas Moore

Traditional Air: "The Old Woman"

There Is Not in the Wide World

Words by Thomas Moore

Traditional Air:
"The Meeting of the Waters"

I Love My Love in the Morning

Words by Gerald Griffin

Traditional Air

Oh! Breathe Not His Name

Words by Thomas Moore

Traditional Air: "The Brown Maid"

The Snowy-Breasted Pearl

Words by Stephen Edward de Vere

Traditional Air: "Pearl of the White Breast"

141

* Darling young girl (pronounced "O gas-tore")
** Fair girl of my heart.

When He Who Adores Thee

Words by Thomas Moore

Traditional Air

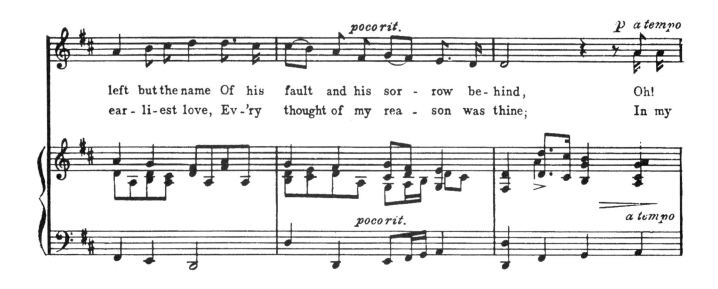

sign'd?   Yes, weep, and how-ev-er my foes may con-demn, Thy
mine!   Oh! bless'd are the lov-ers and friends who shall live The

tears shall ef - face their de - cree; For Heav'n can wit - ness Tho'
days of thy glo - ry to see; But the next dear-est bless-ing that

guil-ty to them, I have been but too faith - ful to thee.
Heaven can give, Is the pride of thus dy - ing for   thee.

The Low-Backed Car

Words by Samuel Lover

Traditional Air: "The Jolly Ploughboy"

1. When first I saw sweet Peg-gy, 'Twas on a mar-ket day; With a
2. In bat-tle's wild com-mo-tion, The proud and might-y Mars, With
3. Sweet Peg-gy round her car, sir! Has strings of ducks and geese, But the
4. I'd rath-er own that car, sir! With Peg-gy by my side, Than a

1. low-back'd car she drove, and sat Up-on a truss of hay; But
2. hos-tile scythes de-mands his tythes Of death, in war-like cars; But
3. scores of hearts she slaugh-ters, By far out-num-ber these; While
4. coach and four, and gold ga-lore And a la-dy for my bride; For the

145

Love Thee, Dearest

Words by Thomas Moore

Traditional Air

1. Love thee, dear - est, love thee!
2. Leave thee, dear - est, leave thee!

Yes— by yon - der star I swear, Which thro' tears, a -
No— that star is not more true; When my vows de -

bove thee, Shines so sad - ly fair. 'Tho'
ceive thee, He will wan - der too, A

too oft dim with tears, like him, Like
cloud of night may veil his light, And

rall.

him my truth will shine:_____ And love thee, dear - est,
death shall dar - ken mine._____ But leave thee, dear - est,

love thee, Yes— till death I'm thine.
leave thee! No— till death I'm thine.

D. S. for Verse 2.

Believe Me If All Those Endearing Young Charms

Words by Thomas Moore

Traditional Air: "My Lodging
Is on the Cold Ground"

Andantino

Be - lieve me, if all those en -
It — is not while beau - ty and

dear - ing young charms, Which I gaze on so fond - ly to - day,___ Were to
youth are thine own, And thy cheeks un - pro-faned by a tear,___ That the

change by to - mor-row and fleet in my arms, Like___ fai - ry gifts, fa - ding a -
fer - vor and faith of a soul can be known, To which time will but make thee more

-way.____ Thou would still be a-dored, as this mo-ment thou art, Let thy
dear!____ No, the heart that has tru - ly loved nev-er for-gets, But as

love - li-ness fade as it will;__ And a - round the dear ru - in, each
tru - ly loves on to the close;__ As the sun-flow-er turns on her

wish of my heart Would en - twine it - self ver - dant-ly still!__
god when he sets The same look which she turned when he rose.__

cresc.

f

dim

pp

The Irish Emigrant

Words by Lady Dufferin

Music by G. Barker

I'm sit-ting on the stile, Ma-ry, where we sat side by side, On a
I'm ve-ry lone-ly now Ma-ry, for the poor make no new friends, But

bright May morn-ing long a-go, when first you were my bride; The
oh, they love the bet-ter still the few our Fa-ther sends. And

corn was spring-ing fresh and green, and the lark sang, loud and high, And the
you were all I had, Ma-ry, my bless-ing, and my pride, There's

red was on your lip, Ma-ry, and the love light in your eye. The
no-thing left to care for now, since my poor Ma-ry died. I'm

Come o'er the Sea

Words by Thomas Moore

Traditional Air

Come o'er the sea,   Maid-en! with me,   Mine thro' sun - shine, storm, and snows!
Was not the sea   Made for the free,   Land for courts and chains a - lone?

Sea-sons may roll,   But the true soul   Burns the same   where - e'er it goes; Let
Here we are slaves,   But on the waves,   Love   and li - ber-ty's all our own; No

153

Too-ra-loo-ra-loo-ral
(That's an Irish Lullaby)

Words & Music by J.R. Shannon

O - ver in Kil - lar - ney,___ Man - y years a - go,___ Me
Oft, in dreams, I wan - der___ To that cot a - gain,___ I

Mith - er sang a song to me In tones so sweet and low, Just a
feel her arms a hug -gin' me As when she held me then. And I

sim - ple lit - tle dit - ty, In her good ould I - rish way, And I'd
hear her voice a - hum - min' To me as in days of yore, When she

give the world if she could sing That song to me this day.___
used to rock me fast a - sleep Out - side the cab - in door.___

retard

REFRAIN *Smoothly with much expression*
in time

"Too - ra - loo - ra - loo - ral,___ Too - ra - loo - ra - li,

mp in time

A Little Bit of Heaven
(Shure They Call It Ireland)

Words by J. Keirn Brennan

Music by Ernest R. Ball

158

said, Sup-pose we leave it, for it looks so peace-ful there! So they
sprink-led it with star dust just to make the sham-rocks grow;— 'Tis the
on-ly place you'll find them, no mat-ter where you go;—Then they dot-ted it with sil-ver To
make it s lakes so grand, And when they had it fin-ished shure they called it Ire-land.—

That Tumble-Down Shack in Athlone

Words by Richard W. Pascoe

Music by Monte Carlo & Alma M. Sanders

The Band Played On

Words by John F. Palmer

Music by Charles B. Ward

Marcia.

Allegretto.

Matt Ca sey formed a so - cial club that beat the town for style, And
Such kiss ing in the cor-ner and such whisp'-ring in the hall, And
Now when the dance was o - ver and the band played home sweet home, They

hire - d for a meet -ing place a hall _____ When
tell - ing tales of love be - hind the stairs _____ As
played a tune at Ca sey's own re - quest. _____ He

lad would have his sweet-heart by his side.——— When Ca-sey led the
march down to the din-ing hall and eat.——— But Ca-sey would not
Ca-sey too has tak-en him a wife.——— The blond he used to

first grand march they all would fall in line, Be - hind the man who
join them al - though ev' - ry thing was fine, But he stayed up - stairs and
waltz and glide with on the ball room floor, Is hap - py miss - is

was their joy and pride,——— For
ex - er - cise his feet,——— For
Ca-sey now for life,——— For

CHORUS.

Valse

Ca - sey would waltz with a straw-ber - ry blonde, And the Band played

165

on, _____ He'd glide cross the floor with the girl he a - dor'd, and the Band

played on, _____ But his brain was so load-ed it near-ly ex-plod-ed, The

poor girl would shake with a - larm. _____ He'd ne'er leave the girl with the straw-ber-ry

curls, And the Band played on. _____

You Can Tell That I'm Irish

Words & Music by George M. Cohan

167

168

169

Give My Regards to Broadway

Words & Music by George M. Cohan

CHORUS.

Give my re - gards to Broad - - way, re -

mem - ber me to Her - ald Square,_____

Tell all the gang at For - ty - Sec - ond street, that

I will soon be there;_____

173

Whis - per of how I'm yearn - - ing, To min - gle with the old time throng,_____ Give my re - gards to old Broad - way and say that I'll be there e'er long._____ long._____

Who Threw the Overalls in Mistress Murphy's Chowder

Words & Music by George L. Geifer

jumped up-on the Pi - an - o and loud - ly he did shout.
we put mu - sic to the words and sung with all our might.

CHORUS.

Who threw the ov-er-alls in Mistress Murphy's chow-der? No bo - dy

spoke so he shout-ed all the louder Its an I - rish trick that's true I can

lick the mick that threw the ov-er-alls in Mistress Murphy's chow - der

The Sidewalks of New York

Words by Charles B. Lawlor

Music by James W. Blake

Because You're Irish

Words by Gustave Kahn

Music by Egbert van Alstyne

1. There's some-thing in an I-rish heart that loves an I-rish song, Of
2. Sure Ire-land's such a ti-ny place to hold so much that's grand, It

I-rish days and I-rish ways they'll sing the whole day long. And
seems to me there ought to be some more of that dear land. And

when you ask me why 'tis you I choose from all the rest, This
in your eyes I see the skies, It's lakes so deep and clear, Sure

lit - tle I - rish song ex-plains just why I love you best.
then it seems I've found a bit of Ire - land o - ver here.

REFRAIN

Sure there's some-thing in the eyes of you, Dear eyes of blue that

shine ____ Some-thing in your voice that thrills me too, When your heart speaks to

180

Ireland Must Be a Garden
(If You Are a Wild Irish Rose)

Words by George Graff, Jr.

Music by Bert Rule

1. Pad-dy asked a girl from Ire-land how she grew so
2. I'd be-lieve most an - y - thing when your eyes start to

fair; "Why, Pat," said she, "they grow like me by doz-ens o - ver there. In
smile, It's eas-y to be - lieve nice things a - bout that bless-ed Isle. I

182

Ireland Must Be Heaven
(For My Mother Came from There)

Words & Music by Joseph McCarthy,
Howard Johnson & Fred Fisher

If You're Irish, Come into the Parlor

Words & Music by
Shaun Glenville & Frank Miller

186

187

The Irish Jubilee

Words by James Thornton

Music by Charles Lawler

1. Oh, a short time a-go boys, an I-rish-man named Do-her-ty, Was e-
2. Cassi-dy at once sent out the in-vi-ta-tions, And
3. Blue-fish, Green-fish, Fish-hooks and par-tridg-es,
4. For des-sert we had tooth-picks, Ice-picks and skip-ping rope, And

lect-ed to the se-nate by a ve-ry large ma-jo-ri-ty, He felt so e-la-ted that he
ev-'ry one that came was a cred-it to their na-tions, Some came on bi-cy-cles be-
Fish-balls, Snow-balls, Can-non-balls and Car-tridges, Then we ate Oat-meal till
washed them all down with a big piece of shav-ing soap, We ate ev-'ry thing that was

went to Den-nis Cas-si-dy, Who o-wned a bar-room of a ve-ry large ca-pac-i-ty,
cause they had no fare to pay, And those who did-n't come at all made up their minds to stay a way,
we could hard-ly stir a-bout, Ketch-up and Hur-ry up, Sweet-krout and Sour-krout,
down on the bill of fare, Then looked on the back of it to see if a-ny more was there, Then the

The Emerald Isle

Young May Moon

Irish Lilt

193

The Kerry Girls

The Rakes of Kildare

Round the World for Sport

194

Royal Irish

Larry O'Gaff

The Humors of Bandon

Strop the Razor

The Tempest

Smash the Windows

The Bunch of Currants

Patrick's Pot

The Growling Old Woman

Top of Cork Road

The Miners of Wicklow

An Irishman's Heart to the Ladies

Jackson's Jig

Paddy Carey

Widow Machree

Kitty of Coleraine

Billy the Barber

Tatther Jack Welsh

Happy Soldier

Full Dress

Old Lougolee

The Connaughtman's Rambles

The Hillside

Catholic Boys

202

The Praties Are Dug

Swallowtail Jig

Joys of Wedlock

Paddy O'Carroll

Kitty of Oulart

Haste to the Wedding

204

Paddy Whack

Irish Washerwoman

Gary Owen

St. Patrick's Day in the Morning

Champion

The Real Thing

206

The Beauties of Ireland

Old Man Dillon

Get Up Old Woman and Shake Yourself

Behind the Bush in the Garden

The Maid on the Green

Shandon Bells

208

Miss Blair's Fancy

The Frost Is All Over

The Clay Pipe

The Joy of My Life

The Sprig of Shillelagh

Trip It Upstairs

Another Jig Will Do

The Rocky Road to Dublin

Drops of Brandy

Fox Hunters' Jig

Triple Jig

Give Us a Drink of Water

The Rakes of Sollohod

214

Lep Up

Moll Roe

Silvermore

Barney's Goat

Honeymoon

The Boy for Bewitching Them

216

Cup of Tea

Emigrant's Reel

All the Ways to Galway

The Bag of Praties

Shule, Shule Agrah

Green Fields of America

The Sixpence

Chorus Reel

The Humors of Castle Comber

Opera Reel

Flannel Jacket

The Devil Among the Tailors

Killdronghalt Fair

Cruiskeen

The Rose

Fairy Reel

The Flower of Donnybrook

Peeler's Jacket

The Wind That Shakes the Barley

Apples in Winter

A Country Dance

Blackberry Blossom

Flogging Reel

Old Crow

Teetotaler's Reel

The Green Fields of Erin

The Galway Reel

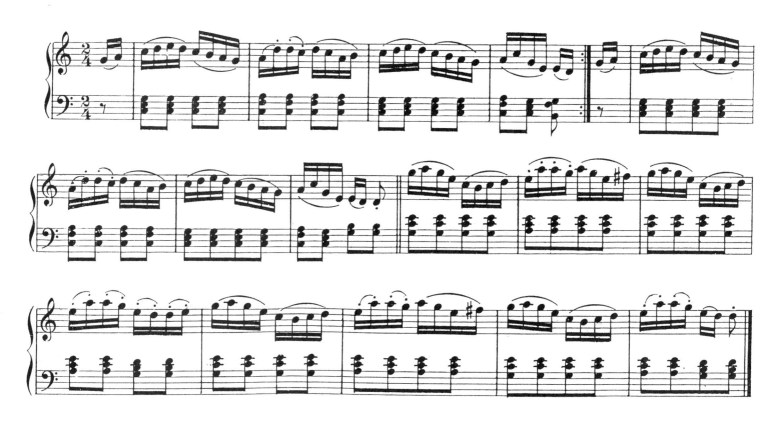

Peter Street

Salamanca Reel

Molly Brallaghan

An Old Reel

Stack of Barley

Guilderoy Reel

Soldiers' Joy

Durang's Hornpipe

Lamplighter

Dick Sand's Hornpipe

Hull's Victory

The Rights of Man

The Redhaired Boy

Liverpool Hornpipe

Rickett's Hornpipe

234

Devil's Dream

The Flowers of Edinburgh

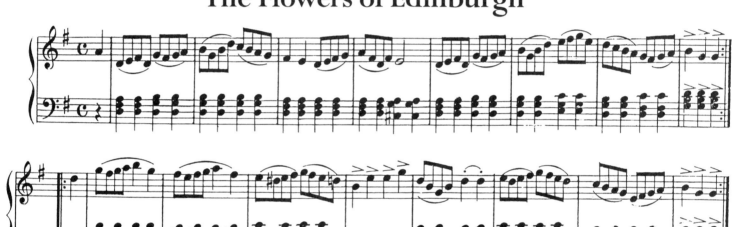

Fisher's Hornpipe

March

The White Cockade

Pretty Lass

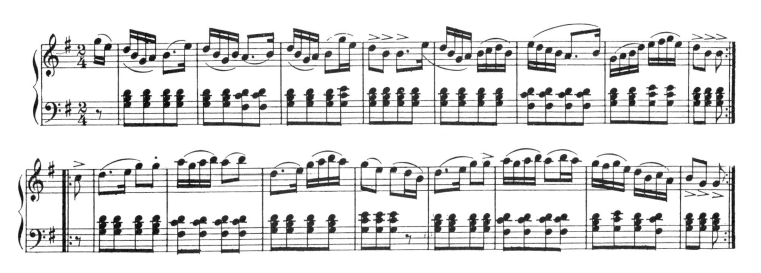

236

Patrick Was a Gentleman

Shamrock

Dawning of the Day

© 1998 Music Sales Corporation (ASCAP)
International Copyright Secured. All Rights Reserved.

The Blackbird

INDEX

Titles in *italics* indicate instrumentals.